Chad Gets Stung

By Clem King

It was a hot day.

Liss and Chad had cans.

A big bug buzzed
to Chad's can!

"My can!" yelled Chad.

"I will hit it with a stick!"
said Chad.

"No, the bug will get mad!"
said Liss.

But Chad hit at the bug
with the stick.

"Stop!" said Liss.
"The bug will sting you!"

The bug sat on Chad's hand.

"The bug stung me!"
yelled Chad.

Liss and Chad ran up
the steps to Mum.

Chad's hand was red.

"Let's put this stuff
on that hand," said Mum.

Liss and Chad sat
on the steps with Mum.

"Where is the bug?"
said Chad.

"It buzzed in the can,"
said Liss.
"So, no more stings!"

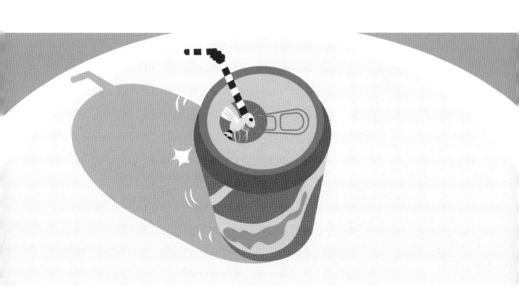

CHECKING FOR MEANING

1. Why did Liss and Chad have cans? *(Literal)*

2. Why didn't Liss want Chad to hit the bug with a stick? *(Literal)*

3. What could Chad have done instead of hitting at the bug? *(Inferential)*

EXTENDING VOCABULARY

buzzed	Look at the word *buzzed*. What is the base of this word? How has adding *–ed* changed the meaning of the word?
sting, stung	What does each of these words mean? Explain that *sting* relates to something that is happening now (present tense) and *stung* relates to something that has already happened (past tense).
stuff	What does *stuff* mean? Can you use it in a sentence? Explain that we often use this word to refer to a group of unrelated items, or something we don't have or know a name for.

MOVING BEYOND THE TEXT

1. Talk about how people can react to stings, i.e. the affected area can turn red and become itchy; some people are allergic and have a more severe reaction.

2. Discuss whether Chad behaved responsibly in this text. What else could he have done?

3. What effect does putting cream or a spray on the sting have? How does it make the area that was bitten feel?

4. What are other ways of treating stings? E.g. putting ice on the area.

SPEED SOUNDS

| bl | gl | cr | fr | st |

PRACTICE WORDS

Stop

stick

sting

stung

steps

stings

stuff